THE SIEGE OF LYME REGIS

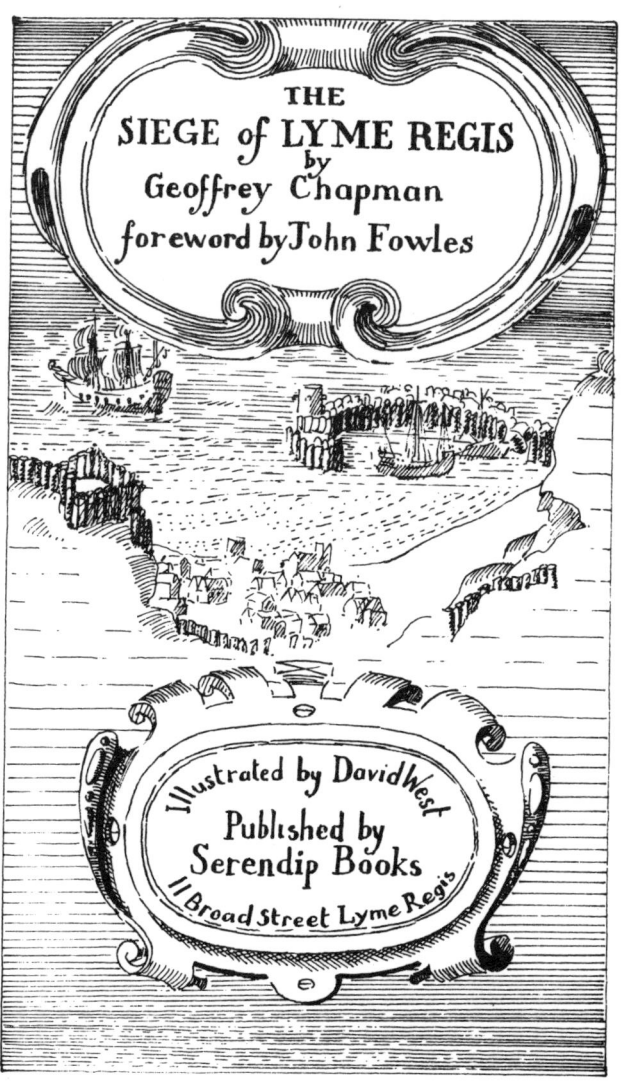

First Published in 1982 by
Serendip Fine Books, 11 Broad Street, Lyme Regis.

© G. M. Chapman, M.A., T.D.

No part of this book may be reproduced in any way whatsoever without prior permission from the publishers.

ISBN 0 9504143 9 5

Typeset and Printed in ten on twelve point Times by Axminster Printing Company, West Street, Axminster.

ILLUSTRATIONS

Model of musketeer	frontispiece
Lyme map	page 10
Joanereidos title page	page 22
"Shot fire arrows"	page 39
Arms of the period	page 46
Reinforcements for Warwick	page 53
Charles I letter	page 57

Figures on page 14, 18, 24 and 31 are courtesy of Hulton Library.

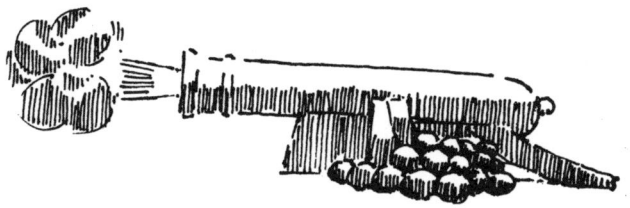

A musketeer of the Parliamentary forces. The men of the Lyme garrison probably looked very much like this. Note the charges hanging from the bandolier and the end of the match dangling from the man's bag.

Courtesy of Worcester City Museum Service. The Commandery Museum.

FOREWORD

By John Fowles

Honorary Curator, Lyme Regis Museum

I am most happy to welcome this addition to the printed history of Lyme. The Siege of 1644 is probably the most famous, and certainly the most characteristic, event in the town's long life; the supreme example of the nobler side of its ancient - and sometimes self-destructive - independent spirit. That spirit, in the form of the Puritan movement, had been dominant in Lyme from the first decade of the 17th century, and we know of only two among the dozen or so important families of the town who followed the Royalist cause in the 1640s. The classic account of the Siege is to be found in A. R. Bayley's *The Great Civil War in Dorset* (1910), which also contains the only published transcript in full of Edward Drake's celebrated diary. But as all local historians know, 'Bayley' is now a rare and expensive book, and Mr. Chapman's skilled version for the less specialist reader fills a marked previous gap in our literature.

Since so much of our information about the Siege depends on Drake's diary, I may perhaps add a word about it. The original manuscript has long disappeared. In 1786 it was found at White Lackington House near Ilminster and shown to Captain Thomas Follett, effectively the first historian of Lyme. White Lackington was owned by the Speke family, who had intermarried with the Drakes, which explains how they came to possess the diary; and Follett's brother Samuel had married a Speke girl, which explains how it came to Thomas's notice. About 1815 he lent the copy he had made to the next historian of Lyme, George Roberts - then only a young schoolboy - who copied the copy. These two transcripts disappeared until 1894, when they were rediscovered, and further transcripts were made of both.

The published version in Bayley was made from one of these later copies, and it varies in many minor ways from the only direct and original one, Captain Thomas Follett's of 1786. The leatherbound commonplace notebook in which it is written, along with many other items, varying from recipes for brewing to a list of the Dorset redcoats who died under Follett's command at Bunker Hill in the American War of Independence, was given to the Lyme Regis Museum in 1921. Who Edward Drake was remains something of an enigma, but he was most probably the gentleman of that name, an attorney of Southleigh in East Devon, who was buried in 1668 at Colyton, and descended from the Drakes of Ashe House, near Musbury.

Those who knew the Siege only through Wanklyn's description of it in the *Retrospect* will note that Mr. Chapman has considerably reduced the perimeter of the town line as proposed in that book. In the absence of archaeological evidence, the exact position of the line and its various forts must remain largely guesswork, but I believe Mr. Chapman's much shorter and 'tighter' rampart is far more likely. What would astound us most today, if we could return to 1644, is how close the two sides lay during those epic weeks - a proximity in static battle that lasted until the trench war of 1914-18. The fighting then, as in 1644, was of course brutal and desperate when men clashed face to face; yet reading Mr. Chapman's narrative, and in this age of the nuclear missile dispatched from thousands of anonymous miles away, I suspect many will feel a kind of envy of how honest - in some strange way almost fraternal - such close-locked warfare was. In this I doubt if 1644 would find much to envy in 1982.

John Fowles.

THE SIEGE OF LYME REGIS

The Civil War between King and Parliament, which began in 1642, initially went well for Parliament in the west of England. In 1643 it veered heavily in the King's favour. By the time Exeter fell in September of that year the Royalists virtually dominated the west from Wiltshire to Cornwall. In the whole of this area only Plymouth, Poole and Lyme Regis held out for Parliament. The exultant Royalists naturally believed that it was only a matter of time before these three strongholds fell to them. Plymouth was already under siege by an army commanded by Prince Maurice, the King's nephew, brother of the more famous Prince Rupert, while Poole was constantly under threat from Royalist-held Weymouth. The danger to Lyme was ominously plain. In 1644 it was still the most important port between Poole and Topsham, making it an attractive prize in Royalist eyes. Furthermore it had a long-established reputation as a centre of radical views in both politics and religion. Mary Tudor had called it "that heretic town" and stopped the annual grant from the Treasury for the maintenance of the Cobb. It was not by chance that, some forty years after the siege, the Duke of Monmouth chose Lyme as his landing place and the starting point of his ill-fated rebellion. He expected to find enthusiastic support there and his expectations were not disappointed. It is significant also that William of Orange, who landed with a large army at Torbay in 1688, lost no time in sending a contingent to Lyme. No wonder that Charles I, in a letter of 11 February 1644 to Sir John Stawell,* the Royalist governor of Taunton, which may be seen in the Lyme Regis Museum, referred to it as "ye rebellious town of Lyme."

Lyme had indeed been asking for trouble. Throughout the first year of the war the garrison had been dispatching raiding parties deep into the surrounding Royalist-dominated countryside. Bridport, Hemyock, Chideock and Colyton had all been attacked in turn and their Royalist garrisons severely handled. People in the wooded hills of the country lying inland from the coast must often have listened with either excitement or apprehension, depending on where their loyalties lay, to the sound of horses' hooves and the jingle of accoutrements as the raiders passed by. To the supporters of the King the town must have seemed a veritable hornets' nest. Early in 1644 the King himself decided that the time had come to settle accounts with Lyme. Prince Maurice was ordered to give up the siege of Plymouth and bring his army east to what seemed the much easier task of reducing the town.

Colonel Thomas Sealey, the Mayor and Governor of Lyme, and Sir Walter Erle, one of the Deputy Lieutenants of Dorset, who had twice been M.P. for Lyme, wrote urgently to Parliament, stressing the danger and asking for help. Parliament authorised them to draw on local funds to pay for putting the town in a position of defence. Work on this had, in fact, been in progress since 1642 and was now intensified, but it was no easy task. Lyme's defences had always faced the sea, the direction from which danger was normally to be anticipated. Defence against an enemy coming from inland had not previously had to

*Reproduced on page 57

be considered. The visitor to Lyme today can see at a glance, as he descends to the town through Uplyme, the vulnerability of its situation, lying in a hollow, dominated by the surrounding hills. In the uncomplimentary words of a pro-Royalist writer of the time, it was no more than "a little vile fishing town defended by a small dry ditch." The word 'vile' had then the meaning of worthless. Even so, to describe a port which had sent two ships to join the fight against the Armada as a worthless little fishing town was a travesty of the truth. The writer of the phrase was nearer the mark with his reference to a small dry ditch. The Lyme garrison had not had time to construct solid defences. Another contemporary writer, Vicars, said of them that they were "so low and thin that in many places one might have run over them - - they being in effect paper on paste-board walls." This was certainly the Royalists' view. They made the fatal error of underestimating their opponents, boasting that the taking of the town was "but a breakfast job" which they would finish before dinner.

To follow the progress of the siege and to understand the problems of both the besieged and the besiegers one needs to try to visualise Lyme as it was in 1644. Compared with modern Lyme it was a very small and compact town. On its seaward side it extended only from the church to Bell Cliff. Inland it stretched little beyond Sherborne Lane and Mill Green. It was bounded on the east by Church Street, on the west by Broad Street, then known simply as East and West Streets. The houses, huddled closely together along the narrow streets, were also small. Sherborne Lane today gives some idea of the town of 1644. Most of the houses were thatched though a few had stone-tiled roofs.

The country around Lyme was more open than it is today. There were not many trees on the hills as they had mostly been cut down for use in building houses and ships. On the Charmouth side lay meadows and sheep pasture. Immediately outside the town however, particularly on the north and west, were many small fields and orchards, known as closes, separated by thick hedges. Such country lends itself to a concealed approach. The Royalists made good use of it to get very close to the town's defences. During the siege the defenders were often aware of their opponents creeping from hedge to hedge, though they could not see them. The Royalists had, of course, one very great advantage in holding the high ground around the town. They could look down onto the defence works and almost into the chimneys of the houses below them. This enabled them to exploit to the full their initial superiority in artillery. It is not surprising that the garrison so frequently sent out raiding parties to try to dislodge the Royalists from their batteries.

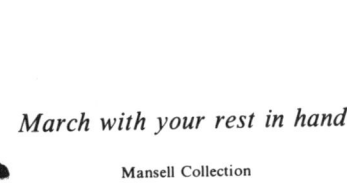

March with your rest in hand

Mansell Collection

THE RIVAL FORCES

The army which Prince Maurice brought to the siege was, on paper, a powerful one. Estimates of its strength vary between 6000 and 2500. Drake put it at 4500. Its main strength was its "excellent trayne of artillery." It was, however, a very mixed force, a fact which was to prove a serious weakness. The core of it was the formidable Cornish infantry, which had so far been on the winning side in all the battles in which it had been engaged. The Lyme garrison certainly held it in respect. Clarendon, best-known of the contemporary historians, wrote that "the Cornish were more terrible to them than any other." In addition to the Cornish there were a regiment of Devonshire men and regiments raised by Royalist supporters such as Lord Poulett of Hinton St. George, near Chard. The method by which some of these regiments were recruited was to prove a source of weakness. They included men pressed into service against their will and so prone to prove unreliable in action, as will be seen in the account of the siege. Finally Maurice's army included a large contingent of Irish and some foreign mercenaries, mainly French. The employment of the Irish and mercenaries caused fierce resentment amongst the supporters of Parliament, not least because they were Catholics, and did considerable harm to the Royalist cause.

Against this polyglot but large and undoubtedly formidable army the Lyme garrison could never muster more than about 1,500 men at its strongest. At the outset of the siege it consisted mainly of Colonel Sealey's regiment of ten companies plus the garrison's cavalry. Re-inforcements of about 230 men were landed from ships of the Parliamentary navy soon after the siege began. Later 300 sailors were put ashore from these ships to join the garrison. However Lyme's defenders, though numerically so much weaker than the besiegers, had one inestimable advantage over them. They were, to a man, in arms by their own choice, resolutely determined to fight for liberties, both political and religious, which they passionately believed to be their rights. For the most part fanatical Puritans, they saw things very much in terms of the Old Testament. Maurice and his army were likened to Sennacherib and his host while they saw themselves as fighting the battles of the Lord, like the Israelites of old. There were said to be no less than twenty-five Puritan preachers in Lyme during the siege, constantly encouraging the defenders and assuring them that any who were killed in the fighting were certain of salvation. It is significant that, while desertions from the Royalist army were, as Drake relates, quite frequent, there were none from the garrison. In Clarendon's words "neither officer nor souldyer, nor any other person, came out of the town (otherwise than upon sallies) to the King's party."

Both sides made great use of artillery. It is interesting to know something of the guns they employed. The heaviest mentioned by Drake was a demi-cannon, brought into Lyme by one of the Parliamentary ships. This monster fired a ball of 32 lbs weight. Otherwise the heaviest guns used by the two armies were culverins (so-named from their snake-shaped handles) and demi-culverins. The former fired a ball of 16 to 20 lbs weight and had an extreme range of about 2,000 yards. The latter fired a ball of 9 to 12 lbs weight and had a range of up to 1,800 yards. Accuracy diminished with increasing range. Culverins were 9 to 12 feet long, had a bore of 5½ inches and weighed about 2½ tons. Most of these guns were made of brass though iron pieces were increasingly used in the later stages of the Civil War. Drake records the landing of both brass and iron cannon from ships. These guns took a great deal of moving. They were dragged along, muzzle first, by teams of horses, harnessed in tandem. They were mounted on platforms, protected by breast-works. The garrison had an advantage here as their guns, once mounted, rarely had to be moved again

A gun crew consisted of three men, the gunner, his mate and a third man to assist them, "to help charge, discharge, mount, wadde, cleanse, scoure and cock the pieces." Thus the loading and firing of a gun took some time. The bigger guns could be fired only ten to twelve times an hour.

Both matchlock and flintlock muskets were used in the Civil War. The Lyme garrison appears to have been armed with the matchlock. This was four feet long, heavy and difficult to handle. It had a range of up to 400 yards but was inaccurate at this longer distance. The round bullet it fired weighed 1¼ ounces and was capable of penetrating a breast-plate. Powder was carried in little tubes of tin or leather tucked in a bandolier. The charge was pushed down the barrel with a gun-stick. A finer type of powder had to be used in the primer or touch-box. This was ignited with a match, a two-feet long piece of twisted tow, pickled in saltpetre, lit at both ends, carried in the musketeer's left hand. To fire the gun one end of the match was inserted in the lock and the pan holding the fine powder opened. Pulling the trigger then forced the match down into the pan. Needless to say it was a slow and cumbersome weapon to use. It also required immense quantities of match as this had to be kept alight all the time. The Lyme garrison consumed a quarter of a ton of match every twenty-four hours. No wonder there was constant anxiety about supplies during the siege.

Cock your match

Mansell Collection

One great advantage the Lyme garrison held over its opponents lay in the quality of its commanders. Sir Thomas Sealey, the Governor of the town, was in titular command, but the real organiser of the defence was Lieutenant-Colonel Blake, who had come to Lyme after Bristol fell to the Royalists. Blake was one of the giants of the Puritan revolution and later of the Commonwealth, an extremely able soldier who later acquired even greater fame as an Admiral. He was undoubtedly the inspiration of the successful defence of Lyme. In addition to Blake there were local men like Colonel Were, Captain Bragg and Captain Pyne and the commanders of the four forts: Davie, Gaitch, Marshall and Newell. These were all leaders of considerable ability, as well as great personal courage. Captain Thomas Pyne, the commander of the garrison's cavalry, in particular deserves to be remembered. The sallies into the surrounding country, on which he led his troopers in the months before the siege began, merit comparison with raids by the Commandos or the Long Range Desert Group in the last war. Had he survived the siege he might have become one of the great cavalry leaders of Cromwell's New Model Army.

The Royalists, by comparison, were poorly led. Prince Maurice was not the equal of his dashing brother, Rupert of the Rhine, lacking his capacity to command and inspire his men. Furthermore he had been seriously ill with influenza, then known as "the new disease." It is possible that he had not fully recovered when the siege began. He must certainly have looked ill for the Parliamentary soldiers joked that the Royalist army was not commanded by Prince Maurice but by his ghost. The subordinate Royalist officers, though unquestionably men of great personal courage, seem generally to have been lacking in military ability. They also had a fatal tendency to disagree amongst themselves.

SEA POWER THE FOUNDATION OF LYME'S SUCCESS

Despite the valour and reputation of the garrison and the townspeople Lyme could not possibly have held out without the support of the navy. The total number of people in the town, combatants and non-combatants, during the siege, was probably about 4,000. They would have been quickly reduced to starvation without the constant supplies of food brought in by sea. Similarly the guns of the forts and the muskets of the soldiers would soon have been silenced for lack of ammunition. In addition there were the reinforcements that came in by sea, not least the valiant sailors lent to the garrison by the Earl of Warwick, the Parliamentary Commander-in-Chief at sea. Indeed the part played by Warwick in the successful defence of Lyme deserves more notice than it sometimes gets. He himself was keenly aware of the desperate situation of the town and its dependence on his ships. It is significant that he remained on one of his ships from his arrival there on May 23rd until the end of the siege.

Official Seal of Lyme Regis.

Joanereidos:

OR,

FEMININE VALOUR;

Eminently discovered in

WESTERN WOMEN,

At the Siege of

LYME.

AS WELL

By defying the merciless Enemy at the face abroad,
as by fighting against them in Garrison Towns; sometimes carrying stones, anon tumbling of stones over the Works on the Enemy, when they have been scaling them, some carrying powder, other charging of Pieces to ease the Souldiers, constantly resolved for generality, not to think any ones life dear, to maintain that Christian quarrel for the long *Parliament*. Whereby, as they deserve commendations in themselves, so they are proposed as example unto others.

With Marginal Notes on the Work, and several Copies of Verses by a Club of Gentlemen on this Authors year and half WORK.

Languet virtus sine adversario.
Horace, *Scribimus indocti, doctiq*; &c.

By *JAMES STRONG* Batchelor, &c.

Re-printed *Anno Dom.* 1674. (with Additions) for the satisfaction of his Friends.

Joanereidos, first published in 1645, was really a lampoon on the Puritan preacher James Strong by his royalist enemies. This is the title page of the 1674 edition.

THE COURAGEOUS WOMEN OF LYME

A notable aspect of the successful defence of Lyme was the active part played in it by the women of the town. Prior to the siege they had helped the men in the digging of the defensive line. During the siege they regularly carried supplies to the soldiers in the forts and the trenches. In his *Memorials,* written in 1732, Whitelocke describes how "the women of the town would come into the thickest of the danger to bring powder, bullets and provisions to the men, encouraging them upon their works." There is a tradition that they wore male attire while on this service in order to deceive the Royalists into thinking that the defenders were more numerous than they actually were. Some of them even stayed to take an active part in the fighting. One woman is said to have fired sixteen muskets at the enemy. After the siege the Reverend James Strong, later Vicar of Ilminster, wrote a poem in tribute to the brave women of Lyme. It is a ludicrously bombastic piece of work but the title pays a well-deserved compliment to those martial Puritan ladies: *"Joanereidos,"* (comparing them all to Joan of Arc) *"or Feminine Valour; eminently discovered in Western Women at the siege of Lyme."* It goes on to enumerate some of the things the women did, "sometimes carrying stones, anon tumbling of stones over the works on the enemy when they have been scaling them, some carrying powder, others discharging pieces to ease the soldiers." One detects a resemblance between these indomitable women and their sisters, staunchly supporting their men-folk in skirmishes with the red men in the woods of New England.

THE DEFENCES

These consisted of a trench, known to the defenders as the Town Line, with an outwards-facing rampart about six feet high, connecting four strong points called forts, though they were more like block-houses, being made of earth, turves, stones and timber. The excavation of the trench, which could have been hardly less than a mile long as it completely encircled the town, must have called for a tremendous effort on the part of the townspeople. Every able-bodied man and many of the women were employed on the work, all of which had to be done with pick and shovel.

No vestige of the defences now remains. They were levelled by order of Parliament in 1647. Any traces of them that might have survived have long ago disappeared, hidden beneath the streets and buildings of the modern town. The course taken by the line and the sites of the forts are therefore uncertain. The positions in which they are marked on the map are

Give fire

Mansell Collection

conjectural, based on evidence discussed below. It is an interesting exercise to walk round the town and decide for oneself where they may have lain, made more enjoyable by the knowledge that one's own guess is as likely to be right as that of anyone else.

The Town Line probably ran from the cliffs east of the church north to a point somewhere near East Cliff, then west to cross the Lim near Mill Green. From here it probably turned south-west to a point near the top of Broad Street from where it ran down to the shore again a little to the west of Bell Cliff. Some authorities think, however, that it lay further inland on the north of the town, following a course close to, and parallel with, the present Woodmead Road.

The most easterly of the forts was Captain Newell's. Drake says that it stood "over the highway leading into the east end of the town." Roberts is more precise. He says that the fort lay "further east of Davie's" (the next fort to the west) and that it "guarded the entrance to the town by Charmouth Lane." This seems to fix the site of Newell's fort with reasonable certainty. There may, however, have been another "way into the town" on the east side, which entered Church Street a few yards above the Guildhall by the narrow passage known as Long Entry. It is possible, therefore, that Roberts might have been mistaken and that Newell's fort guarded this track, not Charmouth Lane. Roberts himself seems to imply the existence of such a track for he writes in his *History of Lyme Regis,* 1834, "Can we ever doubt of persons walking to Charmouth by a footpath many years ago?" Such a track, offering a concealed approach along the cliffs, would have needed to be guarded. There are therefore two possible alternatives for the site of Newell's fort. Both are marked on the map. It will be seen that they both now lie beneath the sea. Coastal erosion has been severe to the east of Lyme. In 1644 the Church Cliffs (known also as the Cleeves) extended at least a hundred yards further out to sea than they do today, providing a flat expanse which was a favourite promenade of the townspeople. This is where Mayor Alford and his friends paced restlessly back and forth through a long June afternoon some forty years later, speculating on the identity of the three strange ships which had anchored offshore, bearing, unknown to them, the Duke of Monmouth and his little band of followers. Nearly all of this expanse has disappeared within the last three centuries.

Eastwards of the Church Cliffs erosion has been even more severe. As recently as 1862 a landslip between Lyme and Charmouth carried nearly ten acres of land, complete with the potato crop growing in it, fifty yards towards the sea. Subsidence still continues here, as Lyme knows to its cost, as it has done for centuries past. It has carried away most of the old Charmouth Lane and whatever track led originally into Long Entry. It is not possible therefore, to visualise the lie of the land to the east of Lyme as it was in 1644, much less to suggest where Newell's fort may have stood as both the possible sites now lie beneath the sea.

One slight objection to locating it in old Charmouth Lane, as Roberts did, is that placing it here would have entailed a considerable eastward extension of the Town Line, something the planners of the defences, with their restricted number of defenders, would surely have tried to avoid. It is possible that Newell's fort was a sort of outpost to Davie's fort and lay outside the line. One fact which lends support to this possibility is that the townspeople do not seem to have been greatly concerned by the early loss of the fort, which was rendered untenable by the Royalist guns only a week after the siege began. They were terrified of losing Davie's fort, "the stay of all," held stubbornly on to Gaitch's in the centre of the line and fought like wild cats to keep the Royalists out of the West fort. The ground on the east side of the town was more open than on the other two sides, making a frontal attack less likely here than on the north or west, where the Royalists could approach the line under cover. Certainly they never seem to have tried one here. The commanders of the garrison knew what they were doing and would not have taken the loss of Newell's fort so calmly if it had been a vital link in the defences.

The key fort in the defences was Captain Davie's, known to the townspeople as "the stay of all." In a characteristic phrase Drake gives the reason for this: "It commandeth round about the town and doth good execution." In other words it occupied a site from which its guns could fire, not only on the Royalist positions on the high ground encircling the town, but on any part of the defences that might come under attack. Drake provides two other clues to the possible site of this fort. In his diary for April 26th he noted that two ships arrived off Lyme and "came in under the command of Captain Davie's Fort." This suggests that the guns of the fort could be brought to bear over the sea approaches to Lyme as well as "round about the town." On May 15th he recorded that "the townsmen began a new platform in the Cleeves between Captain Davie's Fort and the Church." (This platform would have been for guns. It may have been intended to replace Newell's fort.) In attempting to locate a possible site for Davie's fort one must look, therefore, for a position not far from the church, which provides a wide field of fire as described by Drake. North of the church and trending inland is a shelf of gently rising ground. From almost anywhere upon it there is a wide prospect over the hollow in which the older part of the town lies. In 1644, when there were probably few, if any, houses beyond the end of Church Street, this prospect must have been even more extensive than it is today. It seems likely that it was somewhere on this shelf that Davie's fort stood.

Roberts states that Davie's fort was situated near East Cliff Cottage. This apparently stood near the town end of the lane now called East Cliff, though it has had other names in the past. It enters Church Street by the Tudbold Almshouses, a little way above the London Inn. Reference to the map will show that it is all that is left of the old Charmouth Lane, once the main way from Lyme to Charmouth. There is now no single dwelling with the name of East Cliff but the present row of cottages may mark its site and be a pointer to that of the fort. The ground to the north of them is a little higher and provides a better vantage point. This may be where Davie's fort stood.

West of Davie's fort was Gaitch's, sometimes known as the Middle fort. It was sited so as to command the valley of the Lim and the important track which ran beside the river from Colway Bridge.

It could also provide enfilade fire on the part of the line which ran uphill in a westerly direction from the fort in case of a Royalist attack on it. A useful pointer in the search for a possible site for Gaitch's fort is that it was extremely vulnerable to fire from batteries the Royalists placed in Colway Meadow and elsewhere on the high ground beyond the present Woodmead Road. These Royalist guns made the fort untenable on at least one occasion during the siege and the defenders had to dig a sort of communication trench to get in and out of it unscathed.

As its main function was to guard the valley of the Lim, Gaitch's fort must have stood somewhere in the vicinity of Mill Green. Roberts stated that its exact situation was unknown but Curtis thought that it stood in Hill Road, where later the old secondary school was built. This is near the present Woodmead Halls. These stand on a large and comparatively flat expanse, most of which is now a car park. Visualising the prospect from this vantage point as it would have appeared in 1644, without any of the houses now standing beyond it, one can see that it would have provided a clear view up the valley of the Lim, which runs almost straight here up to Colway Bridge. A possible clue to the site of Gaitch's fort was the discovery, in 1834, of a cache of bullets on the west bank of the Lim, in a piece of ground called Hatchet, now marked by a house of that name. In 1923 a small store of cannon balls was found in the vicinity. Ten years later, in 1933, considerable quantities of smaller shot were turned up when the tennis courts were being laid behind the Woodmead Halls. Some of these may be seen in the Museum.

The fourth of the forts, Marshall's, later called West fort when its commander was killed, seems to have been sited so as to cover two approaches to the town, one down Haye Lane and its continuation by what is now Silver Street but was no more than a rough track in 1644; the other an entrance to the town from the west. Drake states that this fort had a gate under it "being the way into town." He also wrote that it "serveth well for the securing of the lane going into the town," His accounts of Royalist attacks on the West fort show that they were able to approach it by a narrow, sunken lane, along which they could advance under cover. This could have been Stile Lane, but this leads up from the Cobb, an unlikely line of approach for the Royalists to take and it seems more probable that Drake's "lane going into the town" was Pound Street. This would have been no more than a narrow lane, or track, between fields, in 1644, but, as it led by what is now Sidmouth Road to the old Roman coast road to Axmouth and Exeter, it could well have been the western entrance to the town, over which the West fort stood. Drake provides two further useful clues to the possible site of this fort. In his diary he gives two accounts of assaults mounted from it on near-by Royalist batteries, on 23rd and 30th of April. The first of these leaves no doubt that the assault was made uphill. After the second, Drake relates, "the water which serveth the town" ran red with blood. This "water" must have been the stream which ran down what is now Silver Street, in a stone channel constructed in 1551, well before the siege. Both these bits of evidence point to a site for the West fort at, or near, the end of Pound Street, below the steep hillside traversed by Silver Street, past the

Library. Some authorities think that this fort stood further out of the town, somewhere near the junction of Pound Road and Silver Street. This site would have had the undoubted advantage of being at the top of the steepest part of the slope. It is difficult to believe, however, that the western entrance to the town was here, or that the fort would have been placed so far out of the town.

From the West fort the line ran downhill, probably just west of Broad Street, to terminate at beach level by one of the town's seaward facing batteries. Built in 1627, this stood in front of the present site of a house called Sunnybank, about a hundred yards west of Bell Cliff. The other seaward facing forts were on Bell Cliff itself and Gun Cliff. They were intended to protect Lyme from attack by sea and played no part in the siege.

Prime your pan

Mansell Collection

NARRATIVE OF THE SIEGE

Prince Maurice and his army arrived on the high ground above Lyme on the 20th of April. They were first sighted, by scouts from the garrison, on Rhode Hill, over which, at that time, lay the main track from the north, to Uplmye and Lyme. From here the Royalists advanced to Uplyme Hill where Maurice summoned the town, by means of a trumpeter, to surrender. The garrison returned an emphatic refusal, adding defiantly that they would give no quarter to any Irish or Cornish. Maurice then attempted to overawe the defenders by a display of strength. He deployed his entire army, horse and foot, along the edges of the steep slopes over-looking the town, "In a breast a mile in length or thereabouts," according to Drake. He added that the men of Lyme " were not a jot dismayed" and "shouted to the enemy who answered them with shouting." It must have been an extraordinary scene, David defying Goliath, Goliath deriding David, more reminiscent of battles in Old Testament times than contemporary conflicts such as Marston Moor and Naseby.

These ceremonial preliminaries being concluded Maurice proceeded to set out his army in battle positions. As far as can be ascertained the four Cornish regiments were placed in the centre, north of the town. On their left were the Irish whose lines ran down to the sea, east of the Church Cliffs. On the right of the Cornish, extending in a semi-circle round to the cliffs above the Cobb, were the Devonshire men and Lord Poulett's regiment. These placings must, of course, have been changed during the siege as military necessity demanded. The Royalist batteries were constantly being moved, as the narrative of the siege will show.

Meanwhile the defenders had withdrawn outposts they had placed in Colway Manor and Haye House, the latter after a brief skirmish. Both of these places were used as bases by the Royalists, Prince Maurice making his head-quarters at Haye House throughout the siege. After the summons to surrender and the shouting match between the two sides the Royalists must have been occupied in getting their forces, particularly the artillery, into position and setting up bivouacs. Drake describes how, as darkness fell, the defenders could see the enemy's camp fires twinkling on the hills all around the town. A sharp watch must have been kept in the Town Line that night.

The garrison did not have to wait long for the first Royalist attack, which came soon after dawn the next day. It began with an attempt by the Royalists to seize some cottages that lay outside the town on its western side. The Lyme men quickly perceived the enemy's objective and circumvented it by setting fire to the cottages. The Royalists then attempted to take advantage of the cover provided by the smoke from the burning cottages drifting across their front to launch an assault on the town's western defences. Drake describes how they "came down into the smoak into the closes from hedge to hedge, brandishing their swords, and so crept into ditches and lay very boldly shooting at us every hour the same day with very great courage within very near pistol shot of our line and the Western fort." This description of the action on the first day of the siege gives a good idea of the enclosed character of the ground immediately outside the line and the type of fighting to which it led. It seems as if the defenders could not see their opponents except in brief glimpses, for Drake's account continues: "notwithstanding the hedges and ditches where the musqueteers of the enemy lay very busy" the Lyme men "slew many of them in sight," that is, those they managed to see. The Royalists seem to have maintained their pressure here, for Drake says that the fire of musketry was incessant and went on both day and night.

The next day, April 22nd, the Royalists raised a battery on the high ground to the north-west of the town, possibly somewhere above the point where Woodmead Road joins Silver Street. It was placed so as to bring fire to bear on the West fort which, throughout the siege, the Royalists seem to have regarded as the weak link in the defences. Fire was maintained on the fort the whole of the day and some damage done to it, which is not surprising as Drake says that it was "little more than musquet proof." However the defenders lost only one man, shot in the head while, as Drake wrote, "indiscreetly looking over the works." It is noteworthy that fire from Davie's fort was highly effective in confining the Royalists to their battery during the bombardment.

The spirit of the Lyme garrison was well displayed on the following day when they took the offensive themselves and launched a vigorous sally on the newly-sited battery. Hand-to-hand fighting took place, the Lyme men using the stocks of their muskets to good effect. The sudden onslaught was too much for the Royalist gunners, who fled. The Lyme men pursued them uphill until they encountered the Cornish, who were of different mettle and drove the attackers back in their turn. Even so they returned with about 35 prisoners and some Royalist colours. Standing at the top of Broad Street and looking up to the high ground beyond the houses it is possible to visualise this furious little up-hill charge and admire the courage of the men who made it.

That night the Royalists, plainly determined to exploit their strength in artillery, raised other batteries in Colway Meadow and near-by. Their objective this time was Gaitch's fort at the centre of the Town Line. As already related the fort was so much damaged that the defenders were obliged to remove two of their guns from it, leaving only one in place to provide enfilade fire on the adjacent part of the line in case an attack should follow the bombardment. Drake noted that the two guns removed from the fort were quickly re-sited "on a new platform not far removed from the said fort very convenient to play on the enemy's new battery." The mettle of the defenders who, in Drake's words, "longed to fight with their enemies more than for a good breakfast," was evident again in another sudden sally on one of the new batteries, made apparently on impulse and without orders. Drake relates that the raiders routed fifty of the enemy, killing some of them and seizing 16 muskets, several pick-axes and shovels and a shoulder of mutton. No doubt this item of Royalist fare was welcome to the defenders, who were probably already having to economise on supplies. Drake says that even this early in the siege "powder and shot began to grow short in the town."

Two days later, on April 25th, the Royalists set up yet another battery, which Drake says was in a lane within pistol shot of the West Gate. This lane was probably the same one Drake mentioned in his description of the position of the West fort. The setting up of this battery, he relates, "constrained the Town to barricade the said gate on the inside with earth and stones three or four yards thick to prevent a breach." It was on the next day that Captain Marsh, the commander of the fort, was killed by an unlucky chance shot that entered through a port-hole in the fort walls.

Having failed to inflict more than superficial damage on Gaitch's and Marsh's forts the Royalists turned their attention to Davie's and Newell's. On April 27th the defenders observed that they were busy at work on still another battery, this time on the east side of the town. This was to become the powerful Fort Royal, which remained permanently in position throughout the siege. It may have been situated somewhere near the site of the present football field. The erection of Fort Royal alarmed the garrison greatly as it was obviously designed to bring fire to bear on Davie's fort, "the stay of all" and the key point in the defences. The defenders set to work at once to strengthen the fort. Drake describes how Captain Davie "thickened and lined his fort on that side next to the battery six or eight feet thick." He adds that "after some shot made thence by the enemy the townsmen perceived that it did little damage to that fort upon which they were much comforted." As already related Newell's fort near-by was rendered untenable and had to be evacuated.

Their failure to reduce any of the forts except Newell's seems to have determined the Royalists to make a change in tactics. As Drake wrote: "They had been round about the town as far as they could go for the sea and assayed all ways and means but storming." This they were now about to do. The attack, carried out by horse and foot, took place on April 28th, a Sunday. Drake describes how they "made an offer of storming the town, blew up their trumpets and beat their drums and sounded an alarm round about the town." There is an echo here of the shouting with which the Royalists attempted to overawe the garrison on the first day of the siege. It may also have been designed to bolster the morale of the Royalist foot soldiers, whose hearts were by no means entirely in their work. Drake's diary provides evidence of this: "The townspeople," he wrote "discharged their ordinance upon them with case-shot which did much execution, which the poor soldiers perceiving and loving their lives best would not venture further -- many of them being forced men, and ever and anon the Horse were constrained to beat on the Foot, slashing and hewing them when they were put on any hard service else they would have run away unto their homes." It is not a pretty picture and grimly illustrates the weakness of an army in which there were many men who had been pressed into service against their will or were foreign mercenaries, seeking plunder rather than military glory. Nevertheless it was a hot engagement. "Their firing seemed a continual blaze" wrote Colonel Were. The noise of it was heard by the crews of ships off Portland.

Frontal assault on the defences having failed as decisively as the attempt to batter down the forts the Royalists tried a third method of subduing the obstinate garrison. On the night of April 29th they shot fire arrows into the town, hoping to set the thatched roofs of the closely packed houses alight. No great success resulted from this stratagem either, the townspeople having provided themselves with supplies of water and wet hides beforehand, in anticipation of such an attack. Such fires as were started were quickly doused and no serious damage was done. Nevertheless it is clear from Drake's diary that Lyme was suffering a fairly steady battering from the Royalist guns. Drake usually says that little 'hurt' was done but the superficial damage must have been considerable and there were certainly casualties amongst the civilian population. The people of Lyme endured this seventeenth century 'blitz' with a stubborn courage that arouses the greatest admiration. Shortage of food was another severe test of their resolve. The beleaguered town was therefore greatly heartened by the arrival, on April 28th, of two ships, from which were landed several cannon, ammunition and provisions and reinforcements of 100 men. The provisions, according to Drake, included beef, pork, dried peas, butter, cheese, bread, beer and wood.

Encouraged no doubt by the increase in their strength provided by the reinforcements brought by the two ships the garrison made one of their vigorous sallies on April 30th. This was on the Royalist lines to the west of the town. It seems to have been directed mainly against one of the powerful Royalist batteries that were proving such a dangerous threat to the town, as Drake tells us that the Lyme men "clogged" one of the guns which had been firing on the West fort. In addition they killed or captured a number of the enemy. It certainly seems to have been a fierce

"Shot fire arrows into the town" p 38 "they shot fire arrows into 3 or 4 houses standing by themselves" pp 51-2.

little battle, as this was the occasion, already noted, when Drake observed that "the water which served the town" ran red with the blood of slaughtered Royalist soldiers after it was over.

After the failure of their attempt to storm the town on April 26th the Royalists lay quiet for several days, partly on account of what Drake describes as "turbulent weather." On the 6th of May they tried again. It was a clever and well-planned attack. A thick fog had rolled in from the sea and the garrison had been on the alert all day, expecting the enemy to take advantage of it. However, as evening approached and no attack had been made, the bulk of the defenders in the line apparently decided that it was safe to go off to supper, leaving only sentries to keep watch. The Royalists may have calculated on this happening for, between 7 and 8 o'clock, they stormed the line in three places, crying "Fall on, fall on, the Town is ours, the day is ours!" It was a dangerous situation. One party of Royalists actually reached the centre of the town but were cut off and either killed or captured. Meanwhile the rest of the defenders had raced back into the line, where furious hand-to-hand fighting took place. The attack was eventually repulsed and the Royalists withdrew, leaving behind their scaling ladders, pikes, grenades and many dead and wounded. Maurice is said to have lost his own colours, which were afterwards displayed by the defenders "in their works." It must have been a near thing, however, and more determined soldiers than the Royalists had might have succeeded. They were led with great courage, but it was once again evident that their "common soldiers" were unreliable. According to Drake many of these took advantage of the dark and foggy evening to run away. For the same reason "the Horsemen could not keep them and slash them together as they did in bringing them on." The Royalists suffered severely in this attack, losing about 100 men, possibly more. Amongst the dead were Captain Paulet of West Melplash in Dorset, who died of wounds two days later, and Colonel Blewett of Holcombe Rogus, near Bampton in North Devon, one of Maurice's best commanders. The next day the Royalists sounded a parley and asked for Colonel Blewett's body, which the townsmen had shrouded and placed in a coffin.

This was the occasion of an often-repeated remark by Blake. When the Lyme men handed over the coffin he asked the Royalists if they had any authority to pay for it. On being told that they had not he replied "Take it, we are not so poor but we can give it to you." A sinister mystery has always hung over Blewett's death. Two of the wounds from which he died were found to be in his back. He had the reputation of being a martinet. Was he, perhaps, one of those who "hewed and slashed" the foot soldiers on and did some of them take a murderous revenge?

The failure of their second attempt to take the town by storm seems to have disheartened the Royalists for no further major assault was made by them during the next two weeks. Artillery fire was intensified, however, and it appears that the besiegers had decided on another change in tactics. Parliamentary ships were continuing to arrive off the town, bringing supplies and reinforcements. It was obviously essential for the Royalists to prevent the landing of these if they were to have any hope of taking the town. Their best chance of success lay, as usual, with their powerful artillery. From about the middle of May they were busy erecting a number of new batteries on the cliffs west of the town. These were obviously intended to fire on shipping in the Cobb and to deny use of the Cobb and Cobb Gate, where supplies and reinforcements were landed, to the town. The defenders had observed the Royalist soldiers trundling away some of their guns from their batteries in Colway Meadow, but apparently had no idea where they were being taken. For once they seem to have been taken by surprise when, in the words of Colonel Were, "the ordnance we had thought drawn off began to speak." At least one of the batteries was situated in Holm Bush Fields which then extended from the present Holm Bush car park westwards as far as Ware Lane. Walking over the ground to-day, with the Cobb plain in view below, one can appreciate how defenceless it was. One battery, according to Drake, was "on the very edge of the cliff next to the Cobb."

The response of the garrison to this grave threat was, as might be expected, highly vigorous. Counter batteries, set up on the west side of the defences, maintained a steady fire on the new Royalist positions and a series of determined sallies mounted. A party of men from the garrison even got into Fort Royal on one of these raids, made at dawn on May 18th, driving the Royalists to "their grand quarter" and spiking one of their guns. A simultaneous sally on the west side of the town met with no opposition, the Royalist soldiers having heard the rumpus going on in Fort Royal and prudently departed. The Lyme men were out again the same night, attacking the breast-works the Royalists were erecting to protect the guns sited to fire on the Cobb. They inflicted considerable damage and seized useful stores of muskets, ammunition, mattocks, pick-axes and shovels. Some of the last three items, the Lyme men were interested to find, were marked with C.R. (for Carolus Rex as Drake thoughtfully informs us) and a crown.

Despite these counter measures Royalist gun-fire on the Cobb and the shipping there was intensified. Their guns could not reach Warwick's ships anchored out in the bay, but they could make things extremely hazardous for the small craft that linked them with the shore. On the 22nd of May one of their batteries (where, as Drake says, they had "a very good gunner") sank a small vessel unloading stores at Cobb Gate. Much worse was to follow. Later the same day a party of Royalist soldiers ran down suddenly from their positions on the cliffs, casting "wildfire" into the barges in the Cobb, burning several of them. In Drake's words it was "a very fatal day to the shipping of the town lying in the Cobb."

The situation had become desperate and demanded desperate measures. A party led by Captain Thomas Pyne, "that most valiant man" as Drake called him, the commander of the garrison's cavalry and the leader of those raids deep into enemy territory before the siege began, dashed out from the defences in a furious charge, driving the Royalists from their battery on the cliff edge. They were promptly attacked by a detachment of Royalist horse and foot and driven back in their turn. They lost several men, amongst them Captain Pyne himself, who was mortally wounded and died five days later. His death was an irreparable loss to the garrison. As Drake wrote, in a phrase the more effective for its simplicity: "more ships might be got again, but such a man was rarely to be found." Pyne was buried in the chancel of the church. The men of the garrison honoured his memory with a salvo from their guns and a volley of shot "fired round about the town," much to the alarm of the Royalists, who thought it heralded a full-scale attack. John Bunyan, who may have been serving with the Parliamentary army somewhere in England at the time, probably had such men as Thomas Pyne in mind when he created the character of Mr. Valiant-for-Truth, he for whom "all the trumpets sounded" when he crossed over the river into Heaven.

Meanwhile the situation in the town was becoming increasingly grave. There was great shortage of food and ammunition, while the people were in sore need of clothing, particularly footwear. The failure of the attack on the Royalists' cliff-top battery was followed by further fire raids on the shipping in the Cobb. An attempt by the Lyme men to tow out one of the unburnt barges was thwarted by the Royalist gunners, who holed the towing boat and killed one of its crew. The rest of those on board plugged the hole with their hats, cut the tow rope and managed to escape. The Royalists promptly came down and set fire to the remaining barges, having first removed from their cargoes anything of use to them. It was fortunate for the town that the Cobb was not then connected with the shore as it is to-day. If it had been the Royalists would probably have taken possession of it early in the siege with consequences impossible to predict.

The fire raids on the shipping there were presumably made at low tide.

The situation at this perilous stage of the siege was saved by the arrival, on May 23rd, of the Earl of Warwick, Lord High Admiral of the Parliamentary navy, with eight ships. It was, wrote Drake in his diary "a great encouragement to our soldiers," who had become so desperate that they had "all resolved to hold out to the last and then cut their way through the enemy." When Warwick came ashore he was appalled at the condition of the town. The sailors from his ships were so affected by the sight of the peoples' plight that they hurriedly collected together a generous quantity of their own rations for them, along with 30 pairs of boots, 100 of shoes and 160 pairs of stockings.

The Royalists, no doubt fully aware of the grim state of affairs in the town, were cock-a-hoop, expecting, as their correspondence shows, to take it any day. With the arrival of Warwick's ships, however, they must have realised that the prize was about to slip from their grasp and determined to make a final onslaught, calling on all their considerable superiority in guns and numbers. They began by intensifying their bombardment of the town and Cobb Gate, where supplies were landed. On the 25th of May, two days after the arrival of Warwick and his ships, they sited more guns on the cliffs west of the town. These, in Drake's words: "played directly on our landing place, so that the town is barred from landing any provisions or necessaries by day." Henceforth all communication between the town and Warwick's ships had to be made during the hours of darkness. Maurice's men must have been very hard at work moving their guns

A matchlock musket of the type used in the siege.
Courtesy of Worcester City Museum Service. The Commandery Museum.

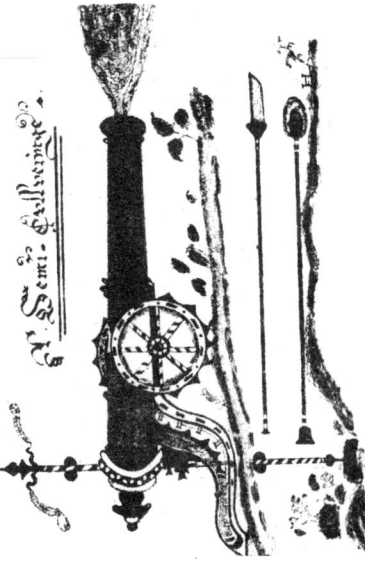

Cannon (demi-culverin) of the period.

about for on May 27th, the day of Captain Pyne's funeral, they began a steady fire on the town, having, in Drake's words: "planted their ordinance so that the enemy's quarters on the west did batter on the eastern quarters of the Town and their east quarters on the Town's western by means the Town situated as in a pit." He says that this bombardment did considerable damage, striking down chimneys and holing the roofs of several houses, besides slaying "several of the garrison about the line." The Royalist gunners seem to have concentrated their fire on their favourite target, the defences about the West fort, where they eventually succeeded in making another breach. However the defenders speedily filled this in and then, in Drake's words: "digged themselves into the ground as in a hole so that at last the ordinance could not hurt them."

In addition to their bombardment the Royalists began a further series of attacks on various parts of the line. These resulted in some of the hottest fighting of the siege, the defenders having a number of men killed and two of their senior officers, Blake and Were, wounded, though fortunately not seriously. Drake says that, in these assaults, the Royalists "came on very thinly but fiercely." He adds, however, that "their common soldiers loving their lives better than such service waited for an opportunity to run away rather than fight." The unusually severe losses suffered by the garrison were mainly from Royalist gun fire, which was maintained throughout the next day, May 28th. This, and the constant attacks on the line, which were clearly the prelude to a full-scale onslaught, probably led Warwick to make a move of the utmost importance.

That night, under cover of darkness, he put 300 of his mariners ashore, to reinforce the hard-pressed garrison. The Royalists, who were perfectly well aware of what was happening, fired off their guns in the general direction of Cobb Gate, but in the darkness their gunners could not see their target and the only damage inflicted was one man wounded. It was the turning point of the siege, in which the crisis was to come within the next twenty-four hours.

The following morning the garrison tried an interesting little experiment in what to-day would be called combined operations. Two ships and six or seven shallops full of soldiers were dispatched eastwards along the coast as if to effect a landing and take the Royalist army in the rear. Maurice's men, suspicious and uneasy, sent a strong party of horse and some foot along the cliffs "to attend the boats." This strategem, devised by Warwick, but in which one also detects the hand of Blake, seems to have been intended to draw off some of the besiegers in order, as Drake wrote, that "they within the town might sally out and fall on the remainder of the enemy." However the Royalists do not seem to have been taken in and soon withdrew the force sent along the cliffs. They were far more concerned about what was happening in Lyme itself. Warwick's sailors had brought several trumpeters with them and they could hear "the sounding of trumpets in the morning about the town." Maurice must have realised that the arrival of the sailors had swung the balance very much in the garrison's favour and determined on a last desperate effort to storm the town. The attack began about midday. It was the beginning of the most perilous few hours in the entire siege for the defenders. The Royalist gunners prepared the way for the onslaught by smashing another breach in the West fort. This was followed by a fierce and determined attack. According to Drake, about 1,000 Royalist soldiers with scaling ladders "came - - home to the breach." Later remarks in his diary seem to imply that, in their approach, they made use of the sunken lane to which reference has already been made.

The battle that followed lasted throughout the afternoon and evening of the long summer day, "even to the setting of the sun very hotly," Drake wrote in his diary. It was contested with great bitterness, the Royalists attacking the breach with desperate courage, the Lyme men - and many of the women - defending it with equal courage, bravely supported by their sailor allies. On that hot May afternoon the interior of the West fort must have been an inferno of noise, dust, smoke and the reek of gun-powder. As often happens in such stubborn contests, where both sides are evenly matched and the issue delicately balanced, an act of individual heroism seems to have turned it in favour of the defenders. One of Warwick's sailors, a man named Moizer, whom Drake describes as "a stout man, both of person and courage," took his stand in the breach "displaying the colours so bravely that out of all doubt he was of great encouragement to the rest of the soldiers, he never giving a foot of ground till such time as the staff of the colours was shot off in his hand, with 2 or 3 of his fingers." Drake describes how he then turned to one of his companions, saying, "Here, take you the colours while I go to the surgeons to be dressed."

Moizer was afterwards decorated and promoted. The story of his brave deed might never have been known, however, but for Drake. Those who stood beside him in the breach would tell their sons and grandsons of him. Some of these would remember and speak of it as an old tale of the siege they had once heard. But gradually it would have been forgotten. It makes one wonder how many other such acts of courage, which turned the tide of battles, have occurred during our history and, lacking a Drake to record them, have passed into oblivion.

This seems to have been the turning point in the battle at the West fort. Royalist casualties had been heavy. Drake wrote that "They drew away their slain almost as fast as they fell," and, at last, were "forced by necessity to retreat into their works and so the storm ceased." He says that the fight lasted eight hours. As the warm dusk of the summer evening descended the quiet in the battered fort must have seemed almost tangible. The relief of the defenders when they realised that they had weathered "the storm," as Drake called it, must have been profound. It had been touch and go. Drake states that "many good shot was made from Captain Davie's fort and platform in the clift during the fight which did very good execution on the enemy as was thought," an interesting example of the power and value of "the stay of all" as well as the range of its guns. Possibly Warwick's seamen, headed by the giant Moizer, had made the difference between victory and defeat, but the indomitable spirit of the men and women of Lyme was the foundation of it. The part played by the women in the siege was never more "eminently displayed," to borrow James Strong's phrase, than in the repulse of the attack on the West fort. Many of them were in the fort itself, filling the soldiers' bandoliers and performing other services. This was the occasion when one of them is said to have fired sixteen muskets herself. Whether this means she fired sixteen separate muskets or sixteen shots from the same one is not known.

The day after the battle was, as might have been expected, a quiet one. The Royalists requested a parley in order to gather up and bury their dead. This was granted on condition that the townspeople had "the pillage of the field" and the Royalists the dead bodies. Such were the rough customs of war in 1644. The men of the garrison took advantage of the respite to repair the breach in the West fort and also to erect a platform above it. This was to guard against any further attempts by the Royalists to make use of the narrow, sunken lane which led to the fort. Drake explains quite clearly why such an addition to the fort's defences was necessary. "This lane being narrow and deep, the enemy may march without danger, five or six in a breast, home to the Line of the Town, which this said platform will prevent." The wonder is that it had not been constructed before.

Following their failure to take the town by storm the Royalists reverted to their previous expedient of trying to burn it down. In this they had some success and might indeed have accomplished their design had the wind been as much in their favour as was the hot, dry weather. On May 31st they shot fire arrows into three or four houses standing by themselves just within the line and burnt them down. It is not known where these houses stood. The next day, June 1st, they did better, burning twenty to thirty houses standing in two streets on the west side of the town. It was fortunate for the townspeople that the wind was from the south, carrying the flames in a northerly direction, out of the town, or the whole of Lyme might have been engulfed by them. The besiegers fired small shot into the burning houses in order to deter the people from fighting the fires. With their customary courage the people continued to combat them and eventually succeeded in putting them out. The soldiers meanwhile were obliged to remain in their defence lines in case the Royalists attacked again. It must have been hard for them to stand and watch the dangerous conflagration, unable to help, but their self-control and discipline were "much admired by them within the town," wrote Drake. Amongst the fire-fighters were a number of Lyme's courageous women, one of whom lost both hands, another an arm, by enemy fire, while carrying water to the burning houses.

On the day before the fire no less than fourteen ships, eight from the east and six from the west, appeared and anchored in the roads off Lyme, alongside Warwick's squadron. They were not bringing supplies, of which the town now had a sufficiency, but the sight of them in Drake's words "much comforted the town." There were now more ships at anchor off Lyme than at any other time in its history, except the 1st of August 1690, when the entire French Channel fleet lay off the town. It must have been a splendid sight. Someone should do a painting of those Parliament ships lying offshore on the summer sea, with the blue wedge of Portland on the horizon. To the

Reinforcements for Warwick.

Royalists the prospect must have been a depressing one. Though they still controlled the Cobb and could prevent ships approaching Cobb Gate during daylight, they could do little to interfere with it at night.

Royalist morale was now very low. Warwick reported to Parliament on June 5th that "The soldiers from the enemy's works seem to have their former spirit and fury much abated, their railing language being not so frequent; nor have the besiegers confidence of their own relief." This opinion was probably derived from the words of two deserters, a sergeant and a corporal, who came into the town that day. They said that the Royalists now despaired of taking the town "so meant to burn it." They also told the townspeople that they had "procured a witch who had undertaken to fire the stone-healed (stone-roofed) houses and furthermore to sink the Lord Admiral with his squadron of ships by devilish art and practice." Drake says that the defenders did remove the thatch from some houses on the east side of the town, but as a precaution of practical nature, "not for fear of the witch or any such devilish practice," as he primly observes.

It is interesting that the two deserters had apparently been much influenced by arguments shouted to the besiegers by the men of the garrison. There seems in fact to have been regular conversation between the two sides during the siege, consisting at first of taunts and challenges but towards the end of the siege, of quite serious discussion.

Despite the evidence of declining morale in the Royalist camp the situation within the town remained grave. On June 12th, only three days before the siege ended, Warwick had written to Parliament emphasising the critical situation in Lyme. The enemy, he said, daily draw nearer, while the garrison is in great need of powder, match and bullets and there are many sick and wounded. His pessimism may have been the result of another serious fire attack on the previous day, when the Royalists shot red-hot bullets and iron bars, crooked at one end, so that they would hang on the houses when they fell upon them. Several more of the thatched houses were, in fact, set on fire by this means, but the townspeople were by now so practised in fire-fighting that they quickly had the fires out. The besiegers also began raising a platform on which to mount cannon, behind an old wall on the west side of the town, within pistol shot of the defences. On June 12th Drake recorded that "the town took notice of it and resolved to remove them thence," to accomplish which they mounted "two great sallies." Drake does not tell us the outcome of this operation, perhaps because he had a very narrow escape from death himself at the time when a shot from a Royalist gun "very narrowly missed myself and some others."

However the end of Lyme's long ordeal was now close. The Earl of Essex, the Parliamentary commander-in-chief, having left General Waller and his army to keep watch on the King in Oxford, had set off westward to relieve the town. The Royalists seem to have had intelligence of this before the townspeople, for another deserter, who came into Lyme on June 13th, told them that the town was about to be relieved and the siege to be raised. The next day a party of no less than 25 officers and men of Maurice's army deserted and came into the town. One of the officers had his wife and her maid-servant with him, a curious example of the domestic aspect of the Civil War. They told the townspeople that the Parliamentary army was not far off and that Maurice was preparing to withdraw his forces. This information was, in fact, inaccurate as regards the Parliamentary army. Essex was no nearer than Blandford. Indeed he never came near Lyme though he may have sent some troops there. Instead he marched off westwards to Exeter and eventually to the disaster of Lostwithiel in Cornwall.

However the Royalists seem to have been convinced that he was close at hand, since the garrison observed that they were taking down their tents and "drawing off their ordnance," though Drake observes that they were still "shooting their fireworks." Captain Davie opened fire from the guns of his fort to speed them on their way and sent out a party of men which "beat the enemy from their hedge works" and chased them back to "their grand battery," presumably Fort Royal. Further evidence of the Royalist withdrawal was forthcoming when ships landing stores at Cobb Gate were fired on only with small shot, the Royalist artillery "being drawn off." The King had written to Maurice as early as May 28th instructing him to leave Lyme if he could not take it. Maurice withdrew to Exeter, which was still in Royalist hands, burning Stedcombe House, the home of Sir Walter Erle, near Axmouth, on his way, "with some loss of reputation for having been so long with such a strength before so vile and untenable a place, without reducing it," as Clarendon wrote.

Though not one of the signatories of Charles I's death warrant, he was too deeply implicated to escape retribution at the restoration of Charles II in 1660 and was executed for high treason. The anniversary of the raising of the siege was observed each year as a day of thanksgiving in Lyme until the Restoration in 1660.

Warwick and many of his officers came ashore and walked round viewing the defences of both sides. "They found those of the besiegers contrived with so much skill and strength, the townsmens' so slight," wrote Warwick's secretary, "that it was a miracle how they could have held out so long against so resolute a foe." Warwick generously gave the credit to the townspeople. "The truth is," he wrote, "the courage and honesty of the officers and soldiers were in a manner their sole defence." None could have known better than he that without the supplies and reinforcements provided by his ships, the town could not have survived. Nevertheless he clearly realised also that a less courageous and resolute people would probably not have held out, even with the support of the Parliamentary navy.

Failure to take the town was a damaging blow to Royalist pride and prestige. Their losses, though not so high as Parliamentary supporters claimed, were undoubtedly heavy. The Royalists themselves said that they were worse than those sustained before either Exeter or Bristol. A letter, found by the soldiers of the garrison on the body of a Royalist officer after the battle at the West fort on May 29th, eloquently expressed the matter from the Royalist point of view.

"That vilainous town of Lyme," he had written, "had destroyed more brave gentlemen of the west and men of honour than had been lost in all the west since these wars began."

The losses of the garrison were amazingly light in comparison, perhaps not much over a hundred. Inevitably there were casualties amongst the civilian population, though these too were not heavy considering the crowded state of the town and the persistent bombardment by the Royalist guns. Drake records a number of deaths of individuals, both soldiers and civilians. These show how deeply the whole town was involved in the siege and how all, young and old, combatants and non-combatants, were equally at risk. One incident he noted was probably typical. "This day Joseph Lanier, an inhabitant of the town, died of a wound received from a piece of ordinance of the enemy's as he was standing in the street...when the enemy had fired the town." Children were equally exposed to danger as a remarkable occurrence recorded by Drake shows. A piece of red-hot iron, shot from a Royalist gun, fell through the roof of a house on to a bed in which five children lay sleeping. Miraculously only one of them was slightly burned. Other entries in his diary tell us more of the people who lived, and sometimes died, in Lyme during the siege. One was a young man named Thomas Way, aged 18, "late a student of the University of Oxon," mortally wounded by the shot which nearly killed Drake himself. Another was a merchant from Bodmin, who happened to be in Lyme by chance when the siege began, stayed to fight with the garrison and, in Drake's simple phrase, "so here ended his life." Typical of the soldiers of the garrison who died was a young man described as "the son of the widow Poole." Even at this distance of time one feels sorrow for the widow, already husbandless and now deprived of a son.

The gunners on both sides seem to have been particularly liable to become casualties. As already explained, it took time to load, lay and fire a gun. During this time the gun crew would be highly vulnerable to retaliatory fire. In any case both sides naturally did their best to knock out their opponents' artillery. The Royalists were said to have lost 27 gunners or their mates during the siege. The garrison's gunners do not seem to have suffered so severely. Drake mentions one, a man named Squires, having an arm blown off. Another lost his life in a most unlucky manner, Drake tells us "as he was washing his feet not far from Cobb Gate." There is a black injustice in this, which affronts the heart, that a man should leave his place of danger in the line only to be killed while performing the comfortable act of washing his feet. Drake noted that some women were drying clothes on the strand near-by. Doubtless some light-hearted badinage was going on. It must have been a tranquil scene, a fit subject for one of the Dutch painters of the time, shattered in an instant by the slam of a gun and the shrieks of the women.

Another of the town's gunners was killed in a curious incident that Drake, with his sharp eye for detail, brings vividly to life. It is worth quoting Drake's account of it in full because of the way it typifies the men of the Lyme garrison. "This very day (May 11th) there were slain in Captain Davey's Fort three men in the evening as they were singing a psalm with the minister at the request of an honest man with a bullet of 18 or 19 pound weight from the enemy's east Battery, one of which was the chief gunner of the Town, all of whose lives might have been saved if they had hearkened to their friends there present who advised them a little before not to sit in that place being on the carriage of one of the guns full in pistol shot." From Drake's account of this episode it appears that the Royalists were certainly able to hear and possibly to see what was to them no doubt a highly sanctimonious performance, a sort of irritating Puritan musak, and decided to put a stop to it. There is no question that the defenders of Lyme allied to dauntless courage a religious fervour verging on bigotry. In an account of the siege in a contemporary Parliamentary news sheet it was stated that "our soldiers sing psalms and pray day and night, having many godly ministers with them."

It is a pity that this conviction of the rightness of their cause sometimes led to intolerance amongst the Parliamentary forces, manifested in acts of needless harshness. Bayley provides an example of this in his account of the cruel treatment meted out by soldiers of the garrison to a Royalist parson, Gamaliel Chase, rector of Wambrook and vicar of near-by Yarcombe. With his wife and seven children Chase was expelled from his parsonage, which was raided on more than one occasion. One of these raiding parties seized Chase's horses and when he pleaded with the raiders to leave him one their response was to mount him on one of his own horses behind the trooper riding it and carry him off to Lyme where he was thrown into gaol. There is also the story of the brutal ill-treatment of an old Irish woman found wandering about in the Royalist lines after the soldiers had gone. She is said to have been put in a barrel and rolled into the sea. It is only fair to say that some accounts of this incident state that it was the work of Warwick's sailors, not the Lyme garrison.

It must also be remembered how severely Lyme suffered from the battering it received from the Royalist guns and from the fire raids. This would naturally provoke feelings of considerable bitterness. The contemporary writer Vicars stated that "there was scarce a house in Lyme remaining undamaged and hardly a room into which shot had not entered." After the siege Parliament ordered that collections for Lyme be made in all parish churches, besides itself voting money for the relief of the town. When the war was over Lord Poulett was directed to make a perpetual payment of £200 a year to Lyme and to provide 2,000 oaks from his estates for the re-building of the town and the replacement of ships destroyed in the siege.

Conditions in Lyme during the siege must have been trying in the extreme, with the normal population of the already crowded little town swollen by recruits to the garrison and refugees from the surrounding countryside. There were also the prisoners brought in from time to time by the raiding parties, though these were got rid of as soon as possible on the ships which brought supplies for the town. Most of the soldiers would have been permanently stationed in the defences but a number of them probably had to be accommodated in Lyme itself. In addition to the soldiers there were the horses of the garrison's cavalry. These would have had to be stabled or kept in picket lines somewhere in the town. The congestion must have been most oppressive in the latter part of May and in June when the weather became very hot. Clarendon, describing the state of Lyme during the siege, wrote, "sickness was very rife there and other exigents which must needs attend a siege - - so long tyme and in the heat of summer, pent so close as that garrison was."

The aggressive spirit of the people of Lyme seems to have been increased rather than diminished by the perils and privations of the siege. Within less than a month of its ending raiding parties were sallying forth from the town again, harrying the Royalists as they had before the siege. The King had given the Parliamentary army under General Waller the slip outside Oxford and was leading his own army west in pursuit of Essex. The country around Lyme was full of Royalist troops, presenting the ferocious little garrison with the sort of targets it found irresistable. On 28th of July a small force of cavalry from Lyme swept into Colyton in the evening and severely mauled a Royalist regiment quartered there. Another party caught the rear-guard of the King's army unawares in Chard. The booty is said to have included eleven of King Charles' own richly-caparisoned riding horses. Later in the year strong forces from Lyme successfully attacked the Royalist garrison in Axminster on two occasions. Axminster suffered quite severely in these raids. Part of the town was burnt and the church tower, where a party of Royalists had barricaded themselves, was badly knocked about by gunfire.

Amongst the leaders of these raids it is with a feeling almost of inevitability that one finds a man named Pyne. This was young Captain Hercules Pyne, later to rise to the rank of Colonel in the Commonwealth army. Whether he was a relative, perhaps even a son, of the great Thomas Pyne is not known. Blake was the inspiration of the defence and the architect of victory; Warwick and his ships provided the supplies and reinforcements without which it could not have been won; but the two Pynes symbolise the valiant spirit of the townspeople, the ultimate foundation of the successful defence of Lyme.

The stubborn resistance of Lyme Regis, Plymouth and Poole had a greater influence on the eventual outcome of the Civil War than is generally realised. These towns not only tied down considerable Royalist forces that might otherwise have been effectively used elsewhere, but greatly heartened the supporters of Parliament in the west of England, which the Royalists almost completely dominated. Devon and Cornwall in fact remained in their hands until the arrival of the New Model Army under Fairfax and Cromwell in 1645. For over a year after the siege ended Lyme remained under constant threat from the strong Royalist forces stationed in the neighbouring towns and villages. The determined attacks made by the Lyme garrison on Axminster and Colyton were designed to cripple enemy units which they knew would otherwise have been employed in further attempts to reduce the courageous little fortress by the sea.

SIEGE OF LYME REGIS
AUTHOR'S NOTE AND ACKNOWLEDGEMENTS

The principal authority I have consulted in writing this account of the siege of Lyme Regis is *"The Great Civil War in Dorset"* by A. R. Bayley, (Taunton, 1910) which contains an almost complete copy of one of the versions of Drake's diary of the siege. Other works to which I have referred are: *"The History of Lyme Regis"* by G. Roberts, (London, 1834); *"The History of Dorset"* by Hutchins, 1869; *"Blake. General at Sea"* by Curtis, (Taunton, 1934); *"Lyme Regis. A Retrospect"* by C. Wanklyn, (London, 1927); *"Blake and the Defence of Lyme Regis"* by the Rev. J. R. Powell which appeared in *"The Mariner's Mirror"* of October 1934. I am grateful to Christopher and Marguerite Chapman of Serendip Bookshop, Lyme Regis, who supplied me with all the above-mentioned books except Hutchins and to the Librarian of Lyme Regis Library who referred me to the article by Powell.

The attempt I have made to suggest whereabouts the Town Line and the four forts may have been situated is based largely on evidence contained in Drake's diary. I hope that the reader will enjoy considering this evidence, perhaps in conjunction with a study of the ground. The map I have drawn to show the possible location of the defences is purely conjectural and may be modified by the reader as he wishes.

In the spelling of personal names I have followed the versions most often used at the time of the siege. Spelling and punctuation in quotations are as in the original sources.

I am extremely grateful to Mr. John Fowles, the Honorary Curator of Lyme Regis Museum, for writing the Foreword to the account of the siege. I am also much indebted to Mr. Fowles and to Miss Muriel Arber for their generous and valuable help. They drew my attention to many details I might otherwise have missed and steered me skilfully round several pitfalls into which I should otherwise have tripped. My sincere thanks go also to Mr. R. G. F. Stanes, M.A., Extra-Mural Lecturer of Exeter University, who read the manuscript and made a number of valuable suggestions for its improvement. I must emphasise, however, that I am solely responsible for the accuracy of the facts stated and all views expressed.

I wish also to thank Major D. C. B. Downe and Mr. N. G. Butler for the time and trouble they took to provide me with some of the illustrations; also the Commandery Museum and the Worcester City Museum Services for permission to use the plates showing a musket and musketeer of the Civil War period. The lay-out, cover design and line drawings are the work of Mr. David West in consultation with the publishers, to all of whom I offer my grateful thanks. The small figures of musketeers are from the Mansell Collection. They are valuable in showing such items of a musketeer's equipment as the musket rest, powder charges and match, which may be seen burning in the musketeer's left hand.

Finally my best thanks go to my sister, Miss E. M. Chapman, who typed the manuscript for me and helped me materially in many other ways.

G.M.C.

Publication List
Serendip, Lyme Regis, Dorset
July 1982: Prices subject to revision

Arber, M. A.
LANDSLIPS NEAR LYME REGIS 60p
(Presidential address, Geologists' Assoc'n)

Chapman, Chris and Clayton, Peter
LYME REGIS WALKABOUT 75p
(Illd. Frances Whistler)
(An affectionate guide to a unique town)

Chapman, Geoff and Young, Bob
BOX HILL Cased, limited and numbered (1000 copies) 3.75
Laminated paperback 2.25
(Naturalists' notes and history of Britain's first Country Park)

Clark, J. Macdonald
THE WITCH OF CHARMOUTH (F) 1.75

Copplestone, Bennet
THE TREASURE OF GOLDEN CAP (F) 1.75

Downe, David
ISANDHLWANA AND ALL THAT 75p
(With the author's brilliant cartoons)

Downe, David and Clayton, Peter
DOWNE ON HIS LUCK 50p
(More cartoons with witty write-up)

Lunt, Jenny and Roper, Sally
SHADOW PLAY 75p
(A year in rhyme with charming silhouettes)

Robinson, Colin
ROCKPOOLING, BEACHCOMBING AND FOSSIL
HUNTING AT LYME REGIS 75p

12 VIEWS OF LYME REGIS & NEIGHBOURHOOD 90p
(Reproductions: originally published c.1840)

Wallace, T. J.
THE AXMOUTH-LYME REGIS UNDERCLIFFS 60p

NOTES

NOTES